AF588284

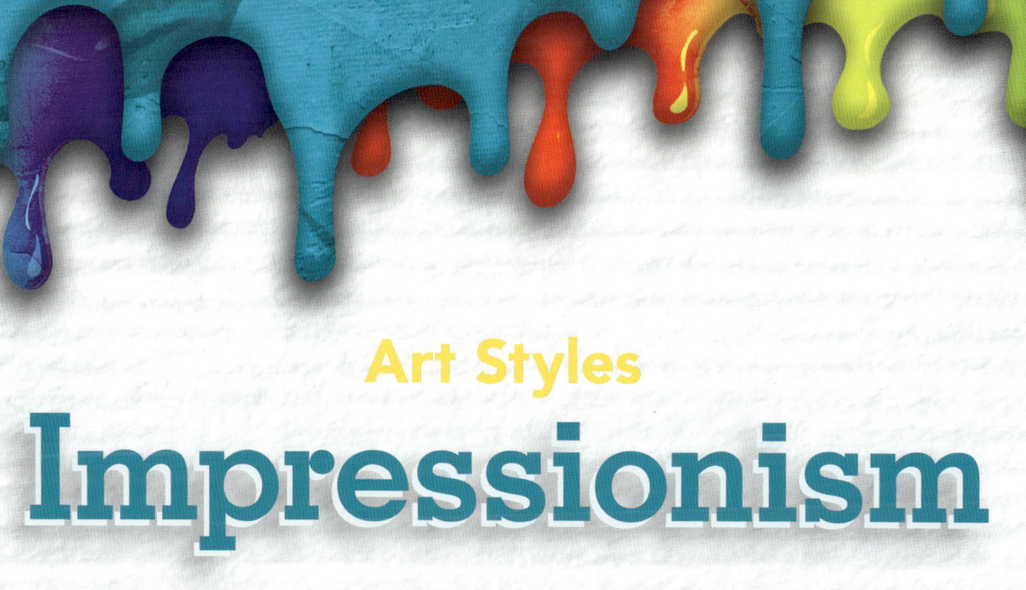

Art Styles

Impressionism

by Julie Murray

Dash!
LEVELED READERS
An Imprint of Abdo Zoom • abdobooks.com

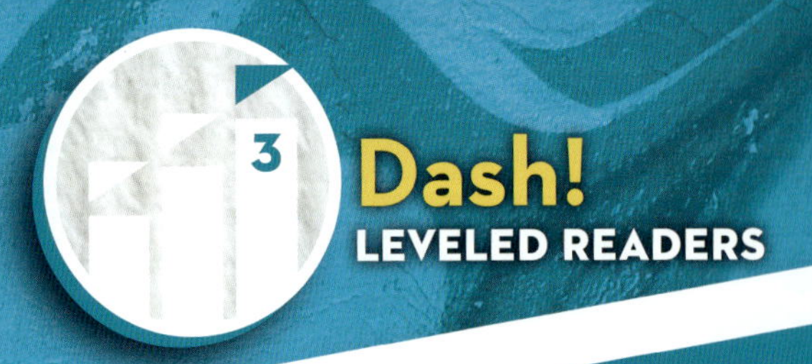

Level 1 – Beginning
Short and simple sentences with familiar words or patterns for children who are beginning to understand how letters and sounds go together.

Level 2 – Emerging
Longer words and sentences with more complex language patterns for readers who are practicing common words and letter sounds.

Level 3 – Transitional
More developed language and vocabulary for readers who are becoming more independent.

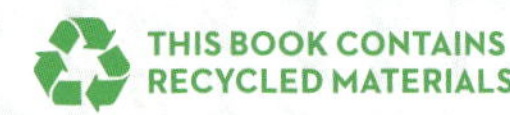

abdobooks.com

Published by Abdo Zoom, a division of ABDO, PO Box 398166, Minneapolis, Minnesota 55439.

Printed in the United States of America, North Mankato, Minnesota.
102023
012024

Photo Credits: Getty Images, Shutterstock
Production Contributors: Kenny Abdo, Jennie Forsberg, Grace Hansen, John Hansen
Design Contributors: Candice Keimig, Neil Klinepier

Library of Congress Control Number: 2023937911

Publisher's Cataloging in Publication Data

Names: Murray, Julie, author.
Title: Impressionism / by Julie Murray
Description: Minneapolis, Minnesota : Abdo Zoom, 2024 | Series: Art styles | Includes online resources and index.
Identifiers: ISBN 9781098283957 (lib. bdg.) | ISBN 9781098284671 (eBook) | ISBN 9781098285036 (Read-to-Me eBook)
Subjects: LCSH: Impressionism (Art)--Juvenile literature. | Impressionism (Art)--France--Juvenile literature. | Art, Modern--19th century--History--Juvenile literature. | Painting--Juvenile literature.
Classification: DDC 759.05--dc23

Table of Contents

Impressionism 4
History 6
Artists 16
More Facts 22
Glossary 23
Index 24
Online Resources 24

Impressionism

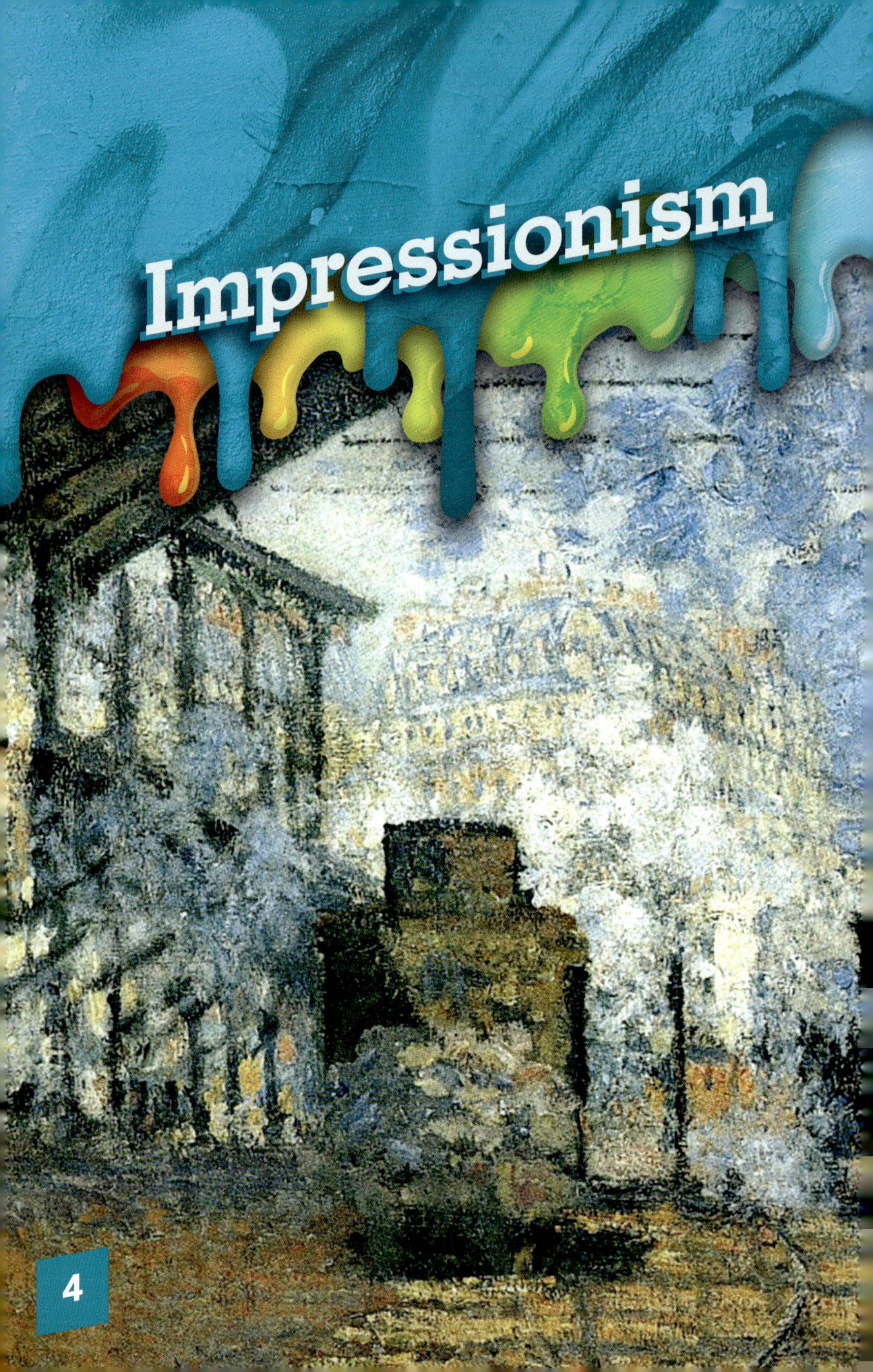

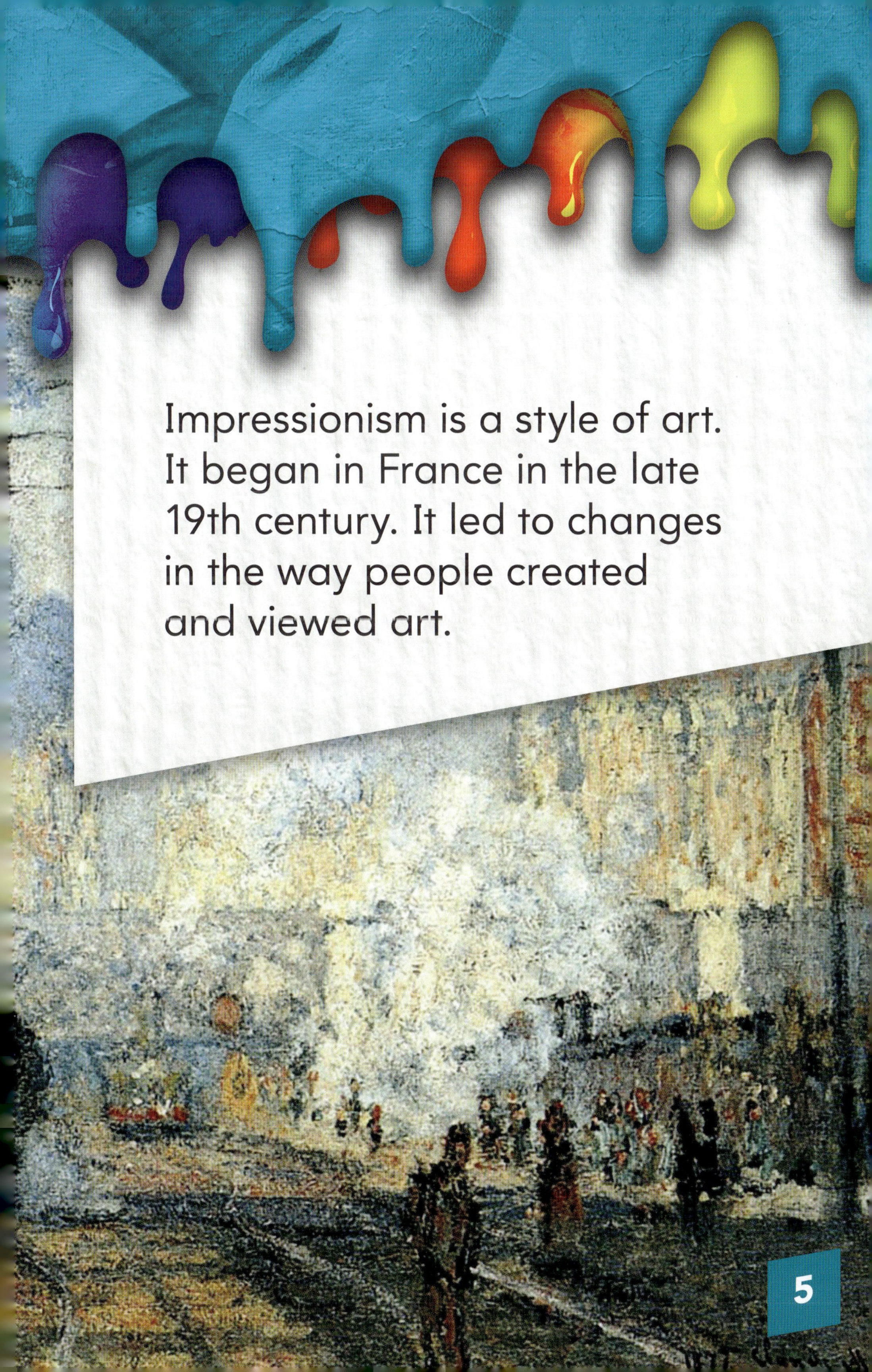

Impressionism is a style of art. It began in France in the late 19th century. It led to changes in the way people created and viewed art.

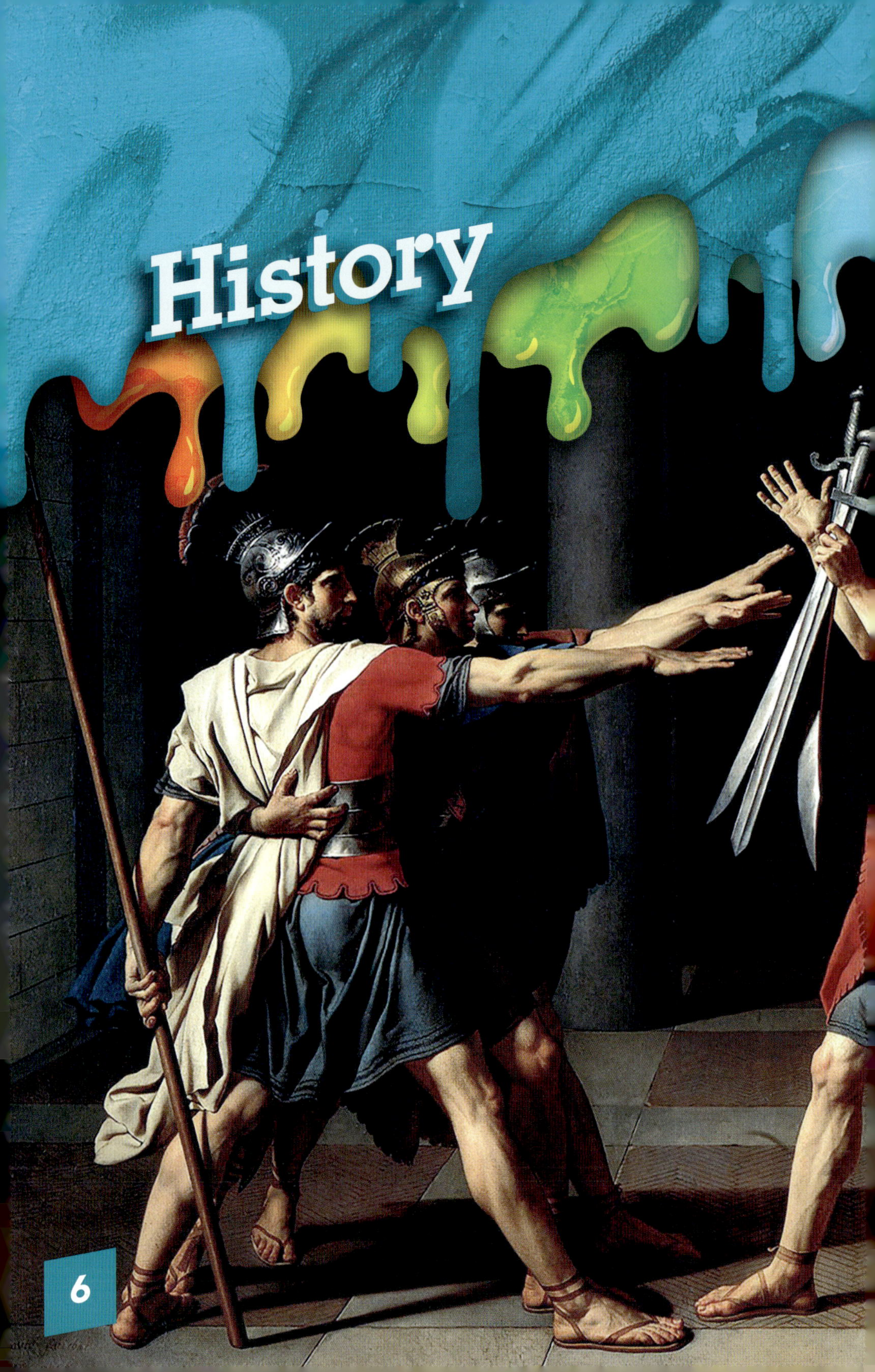

History

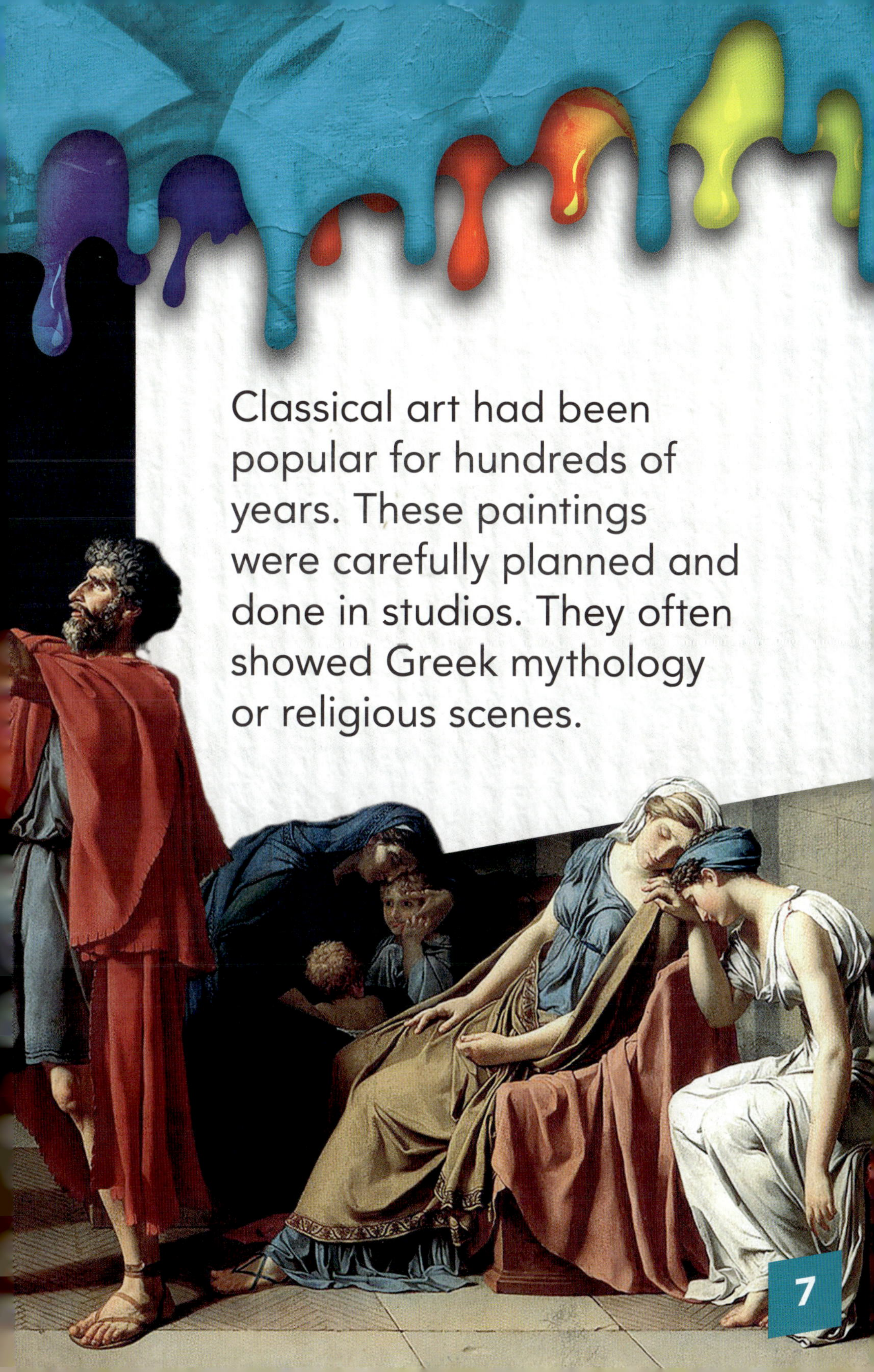

Classical art had been popular for hundreds of years. These paintings were carefully planned and done in studios. They often showed Greek mythology or religious scenes.

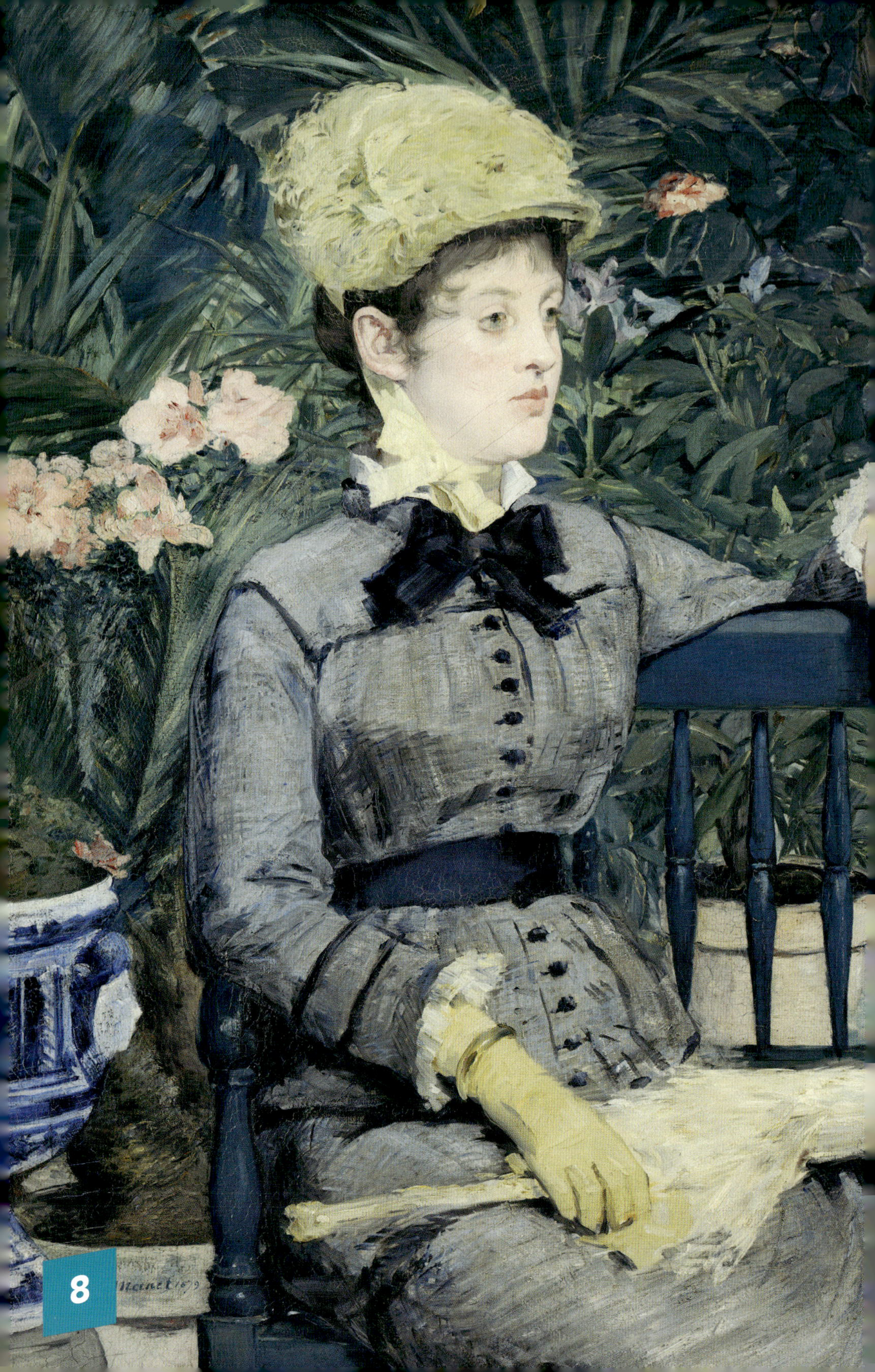
8

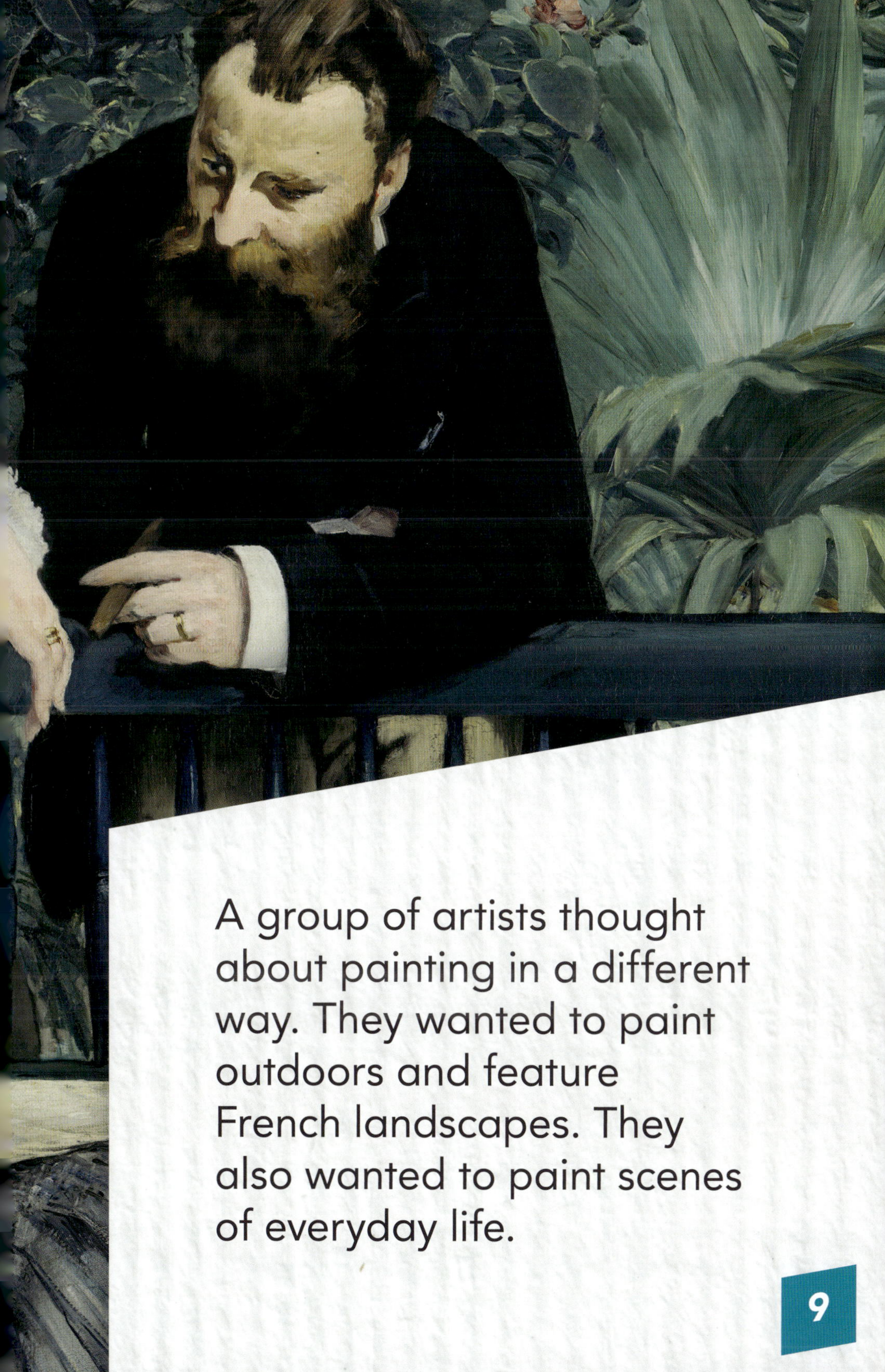

A group of artists thought about painting in a different way. They wanted to paint outdoors and feature French landscapes. They also wanted to paint scenes of everyday life.

This group would become known as Impressionist painters. They used quick, bold brushstrokes. They also used brighter colors than Classical painters.

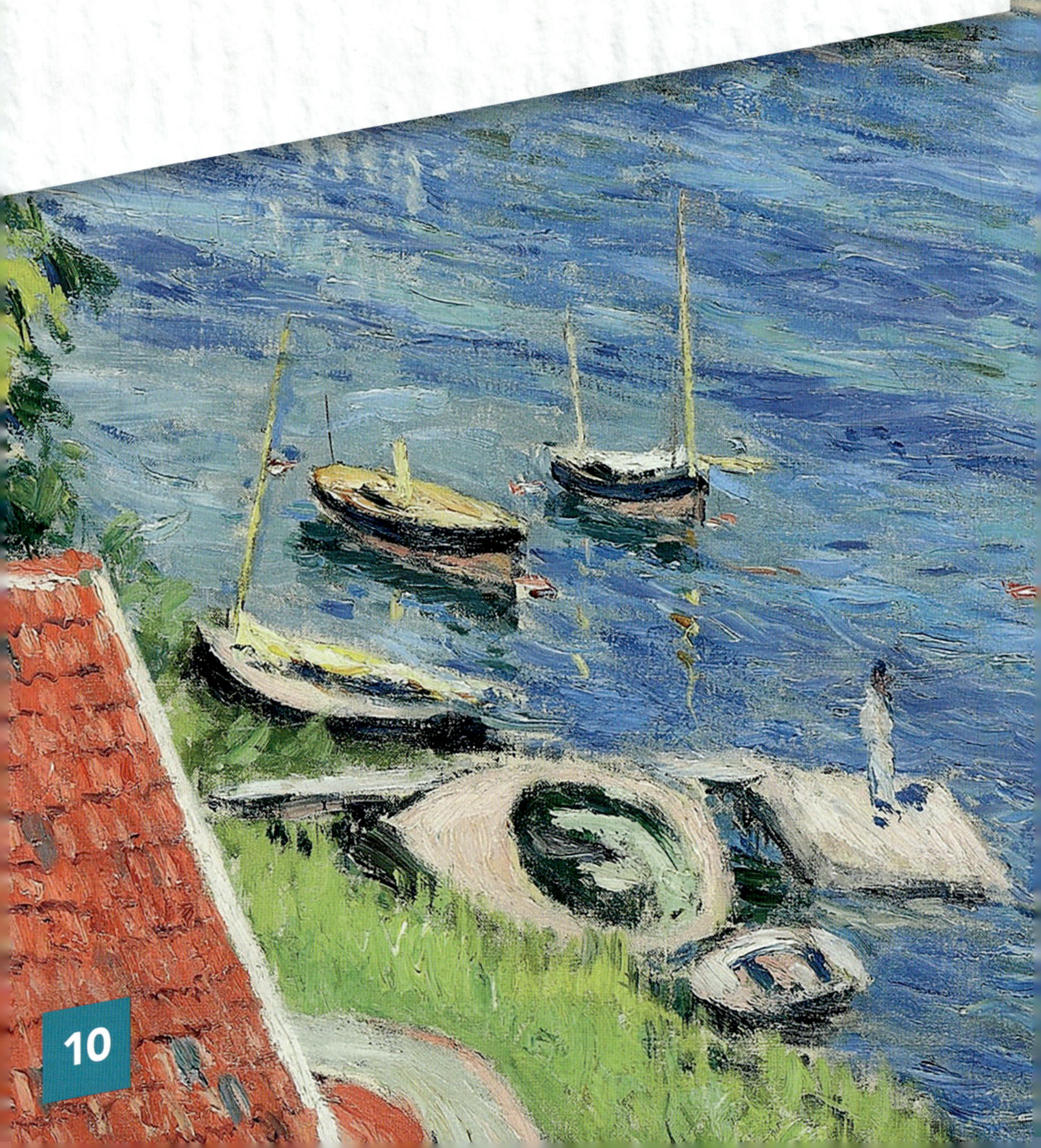

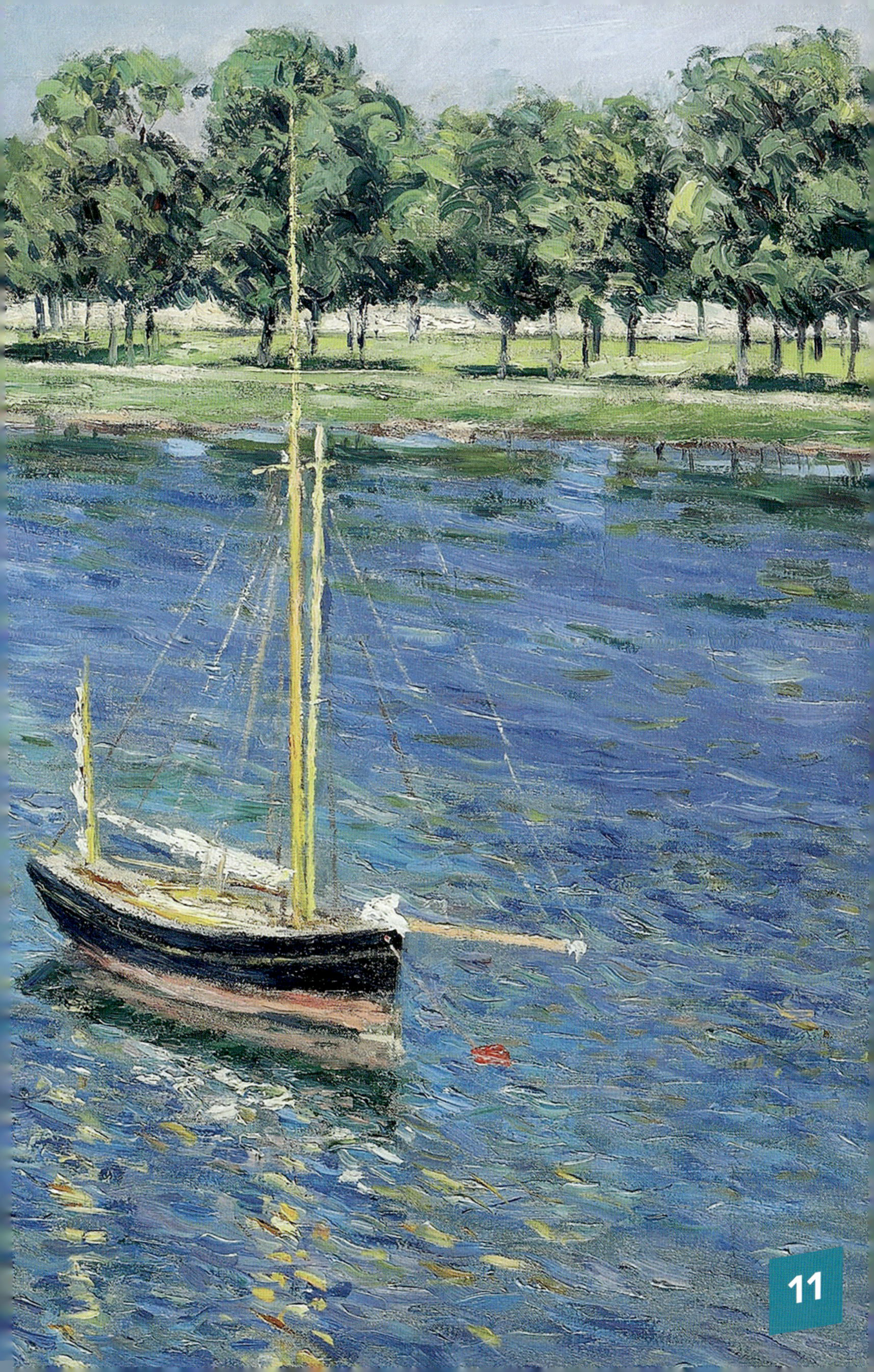

Impressionists paid close attention to weather and light. They often painted the same scene more than once. This showed how the scene changed depending on the weather or time of day.

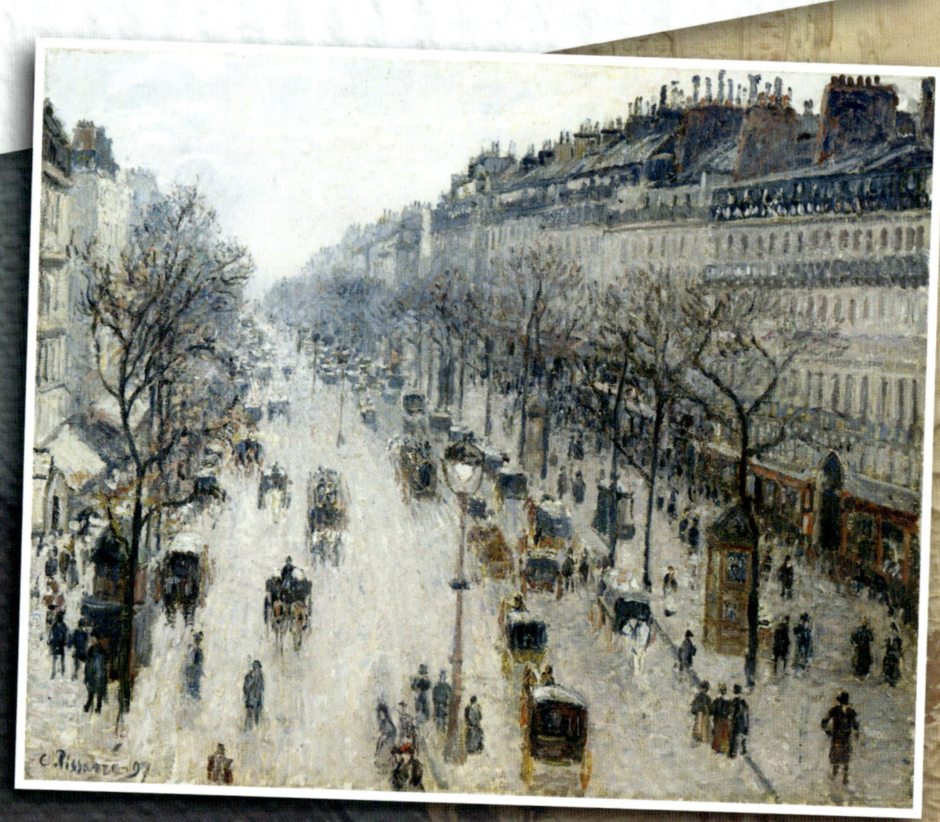

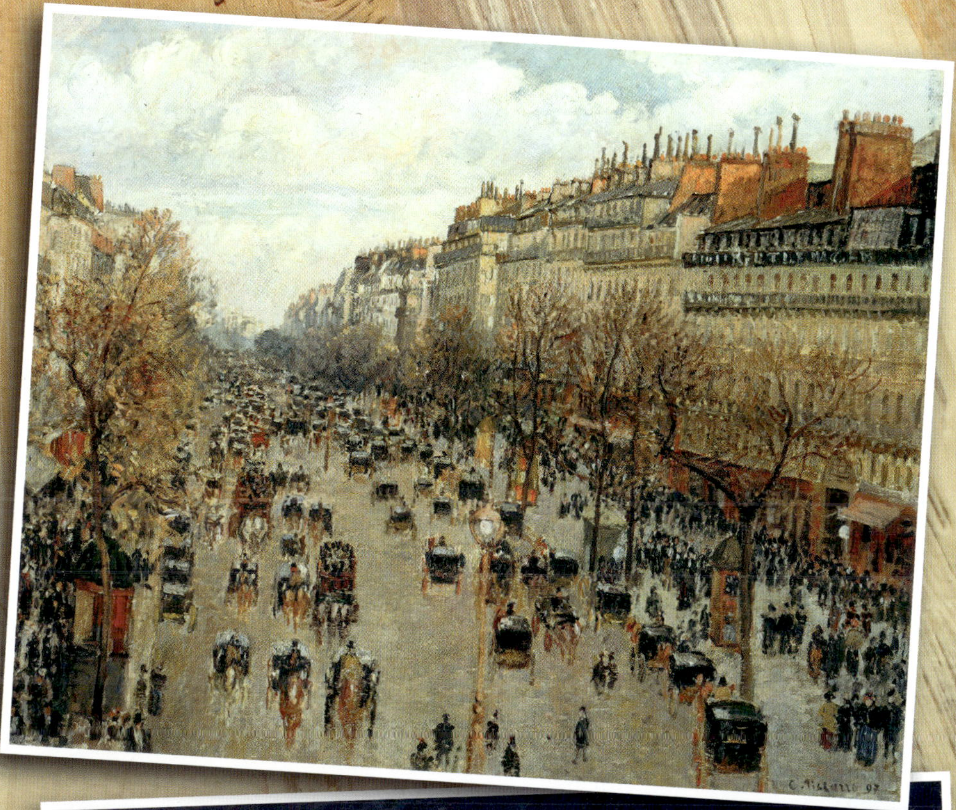

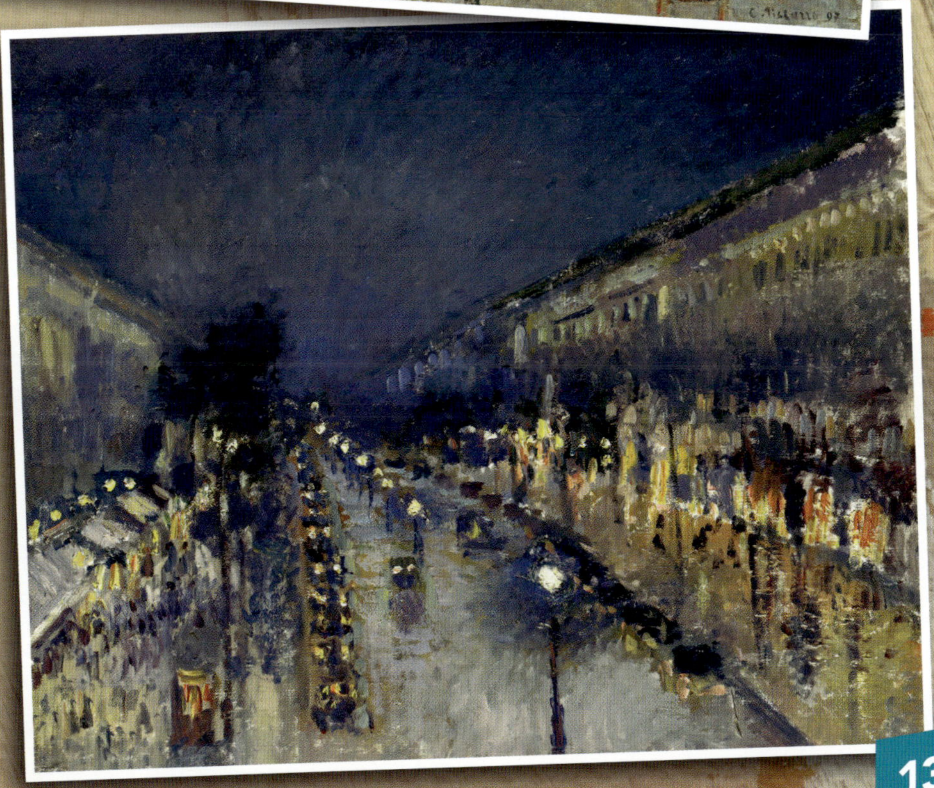

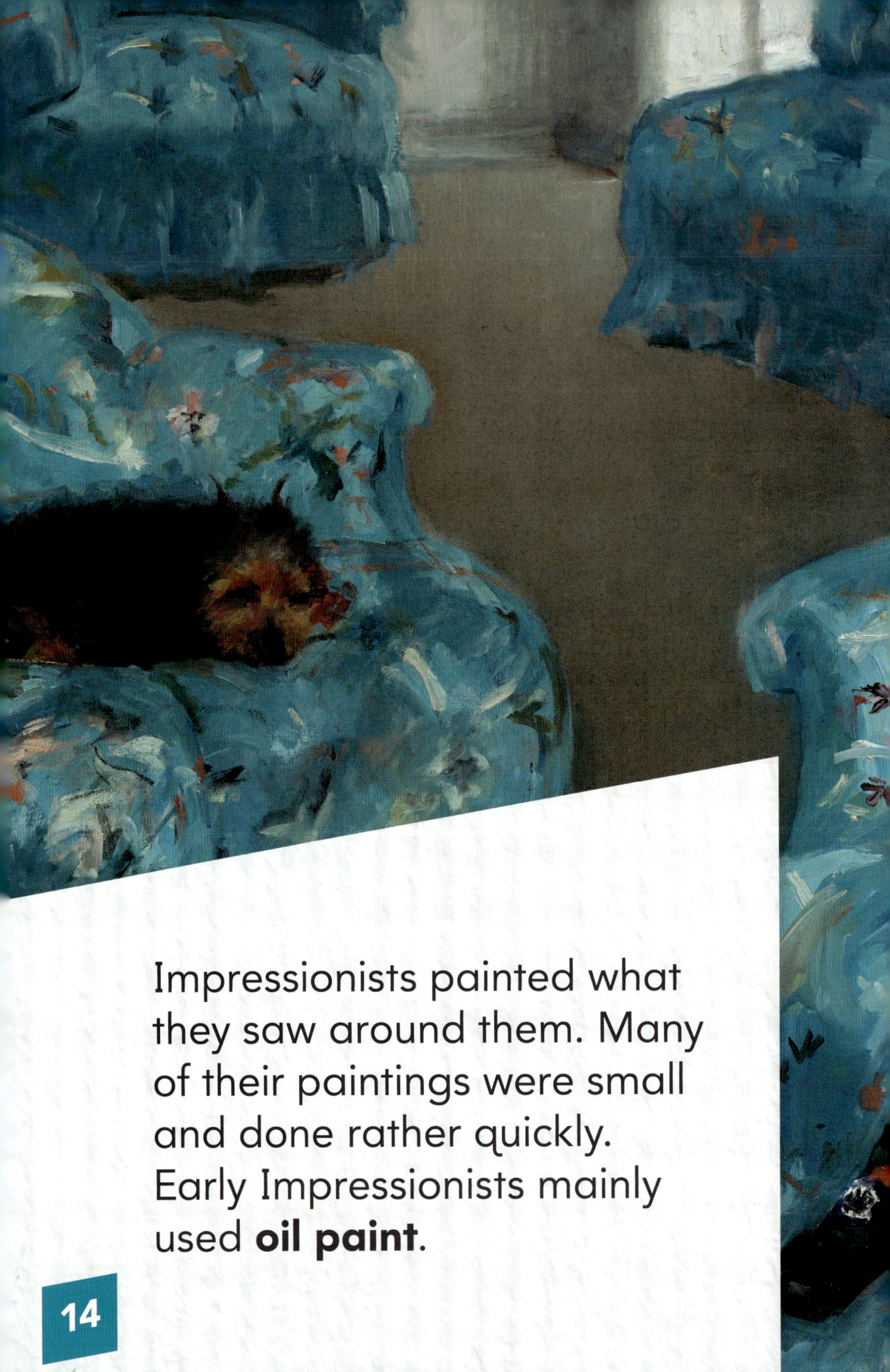

Impressionists painted what they saw around them. Many of their paintings were small and done rather quickly. Early Impressionists mainly used **oil paint**.

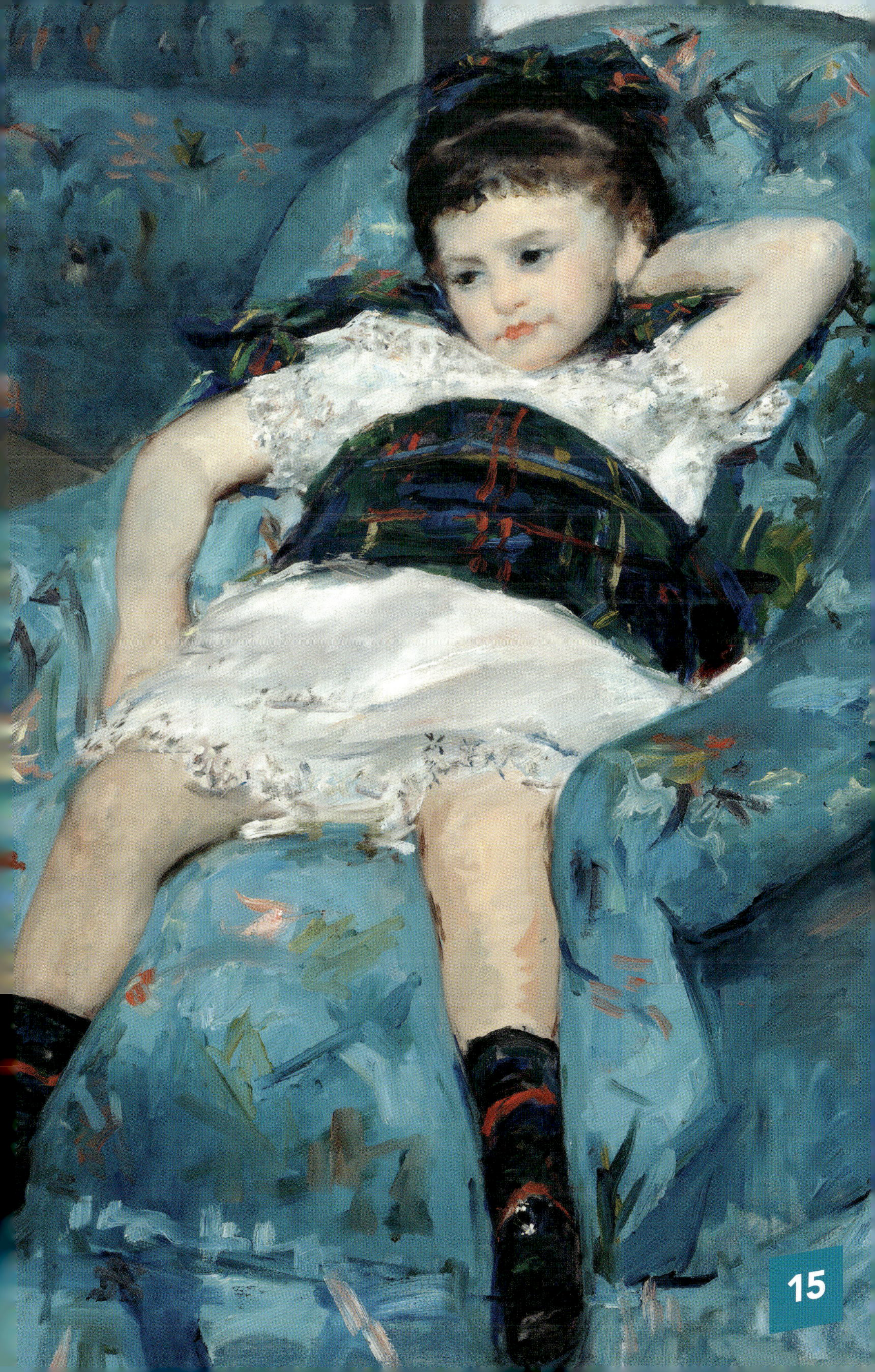

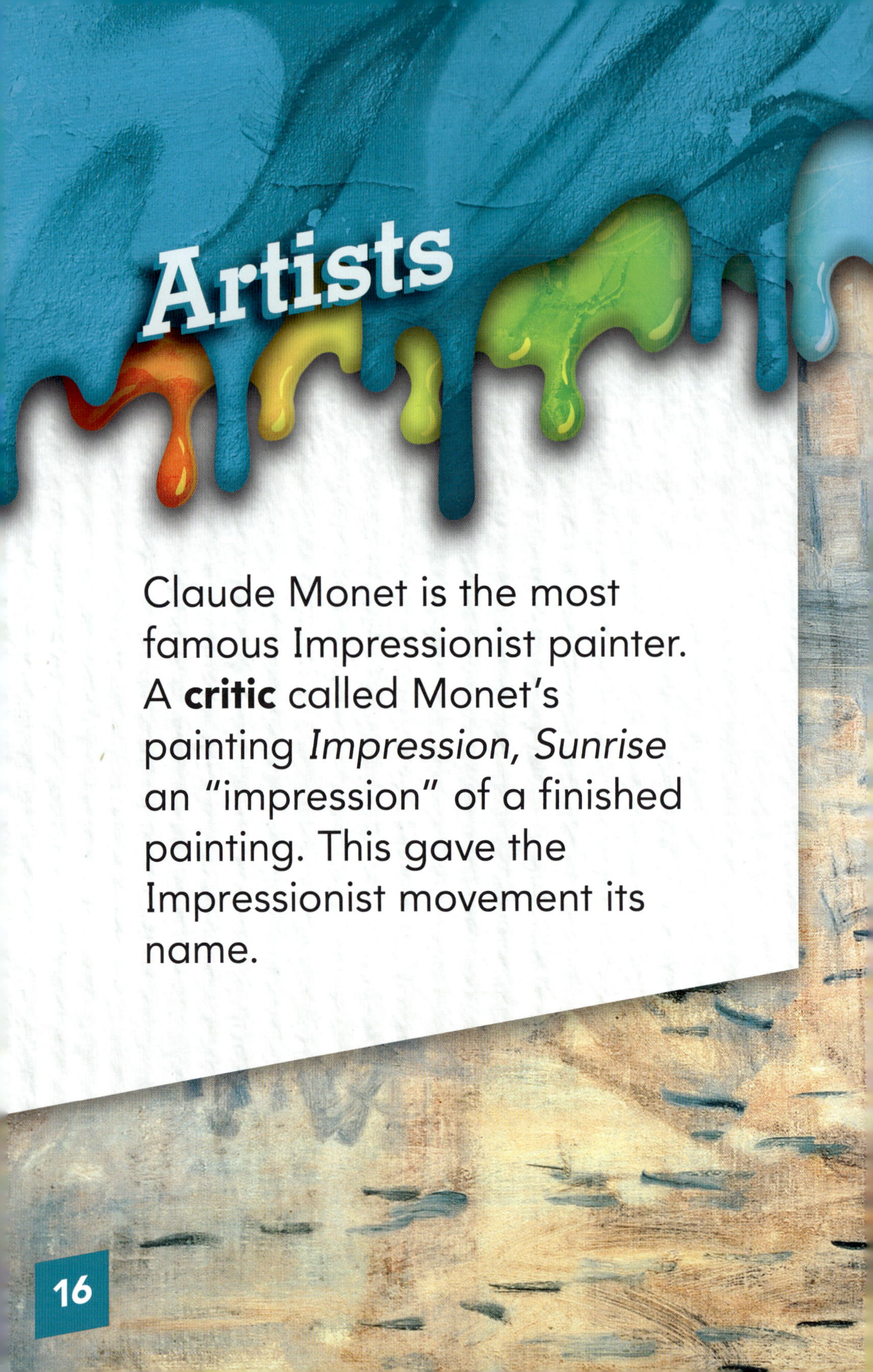

Artists

Claude Monet is the most famous Impressionist painter. A **critic** called Monet's painting *Impression, Sunrise* an "impression" of a finished painting. This gave the Impressionist movement its name.

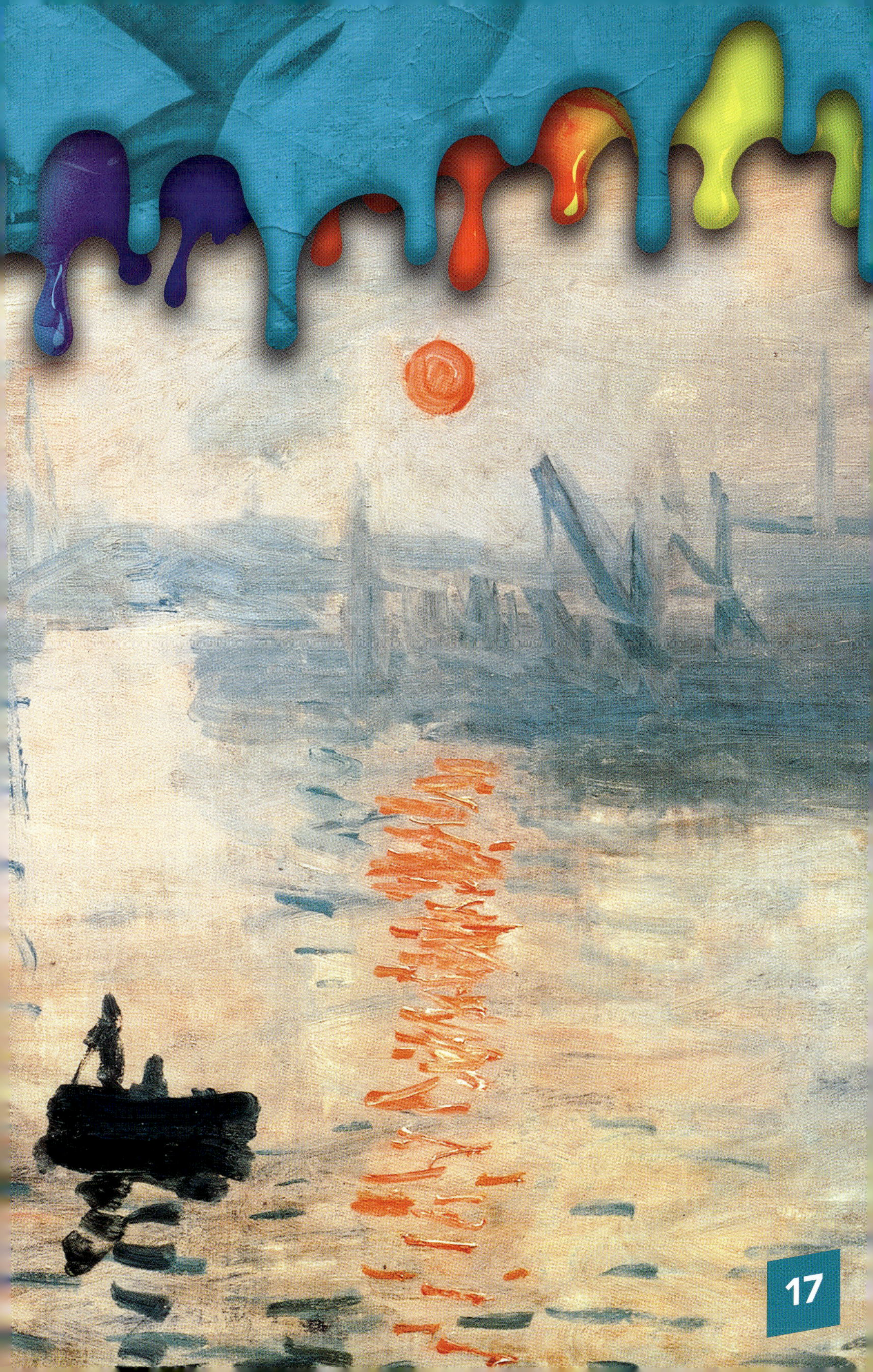

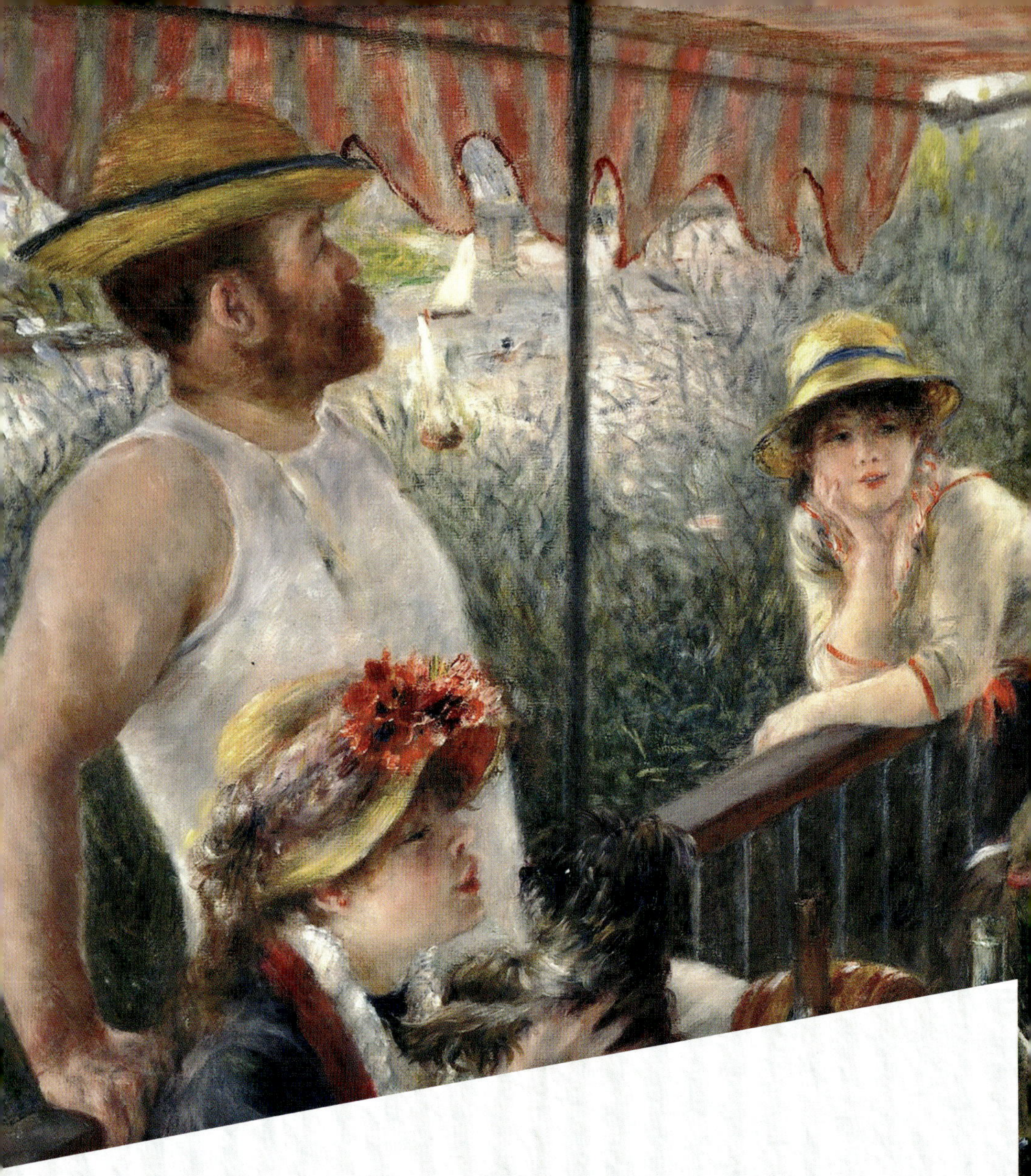

Pierre-Auguste Renoir was a leading Impressionist artist. His painting *Luncheon of the Boating Party* featured many of his friends.

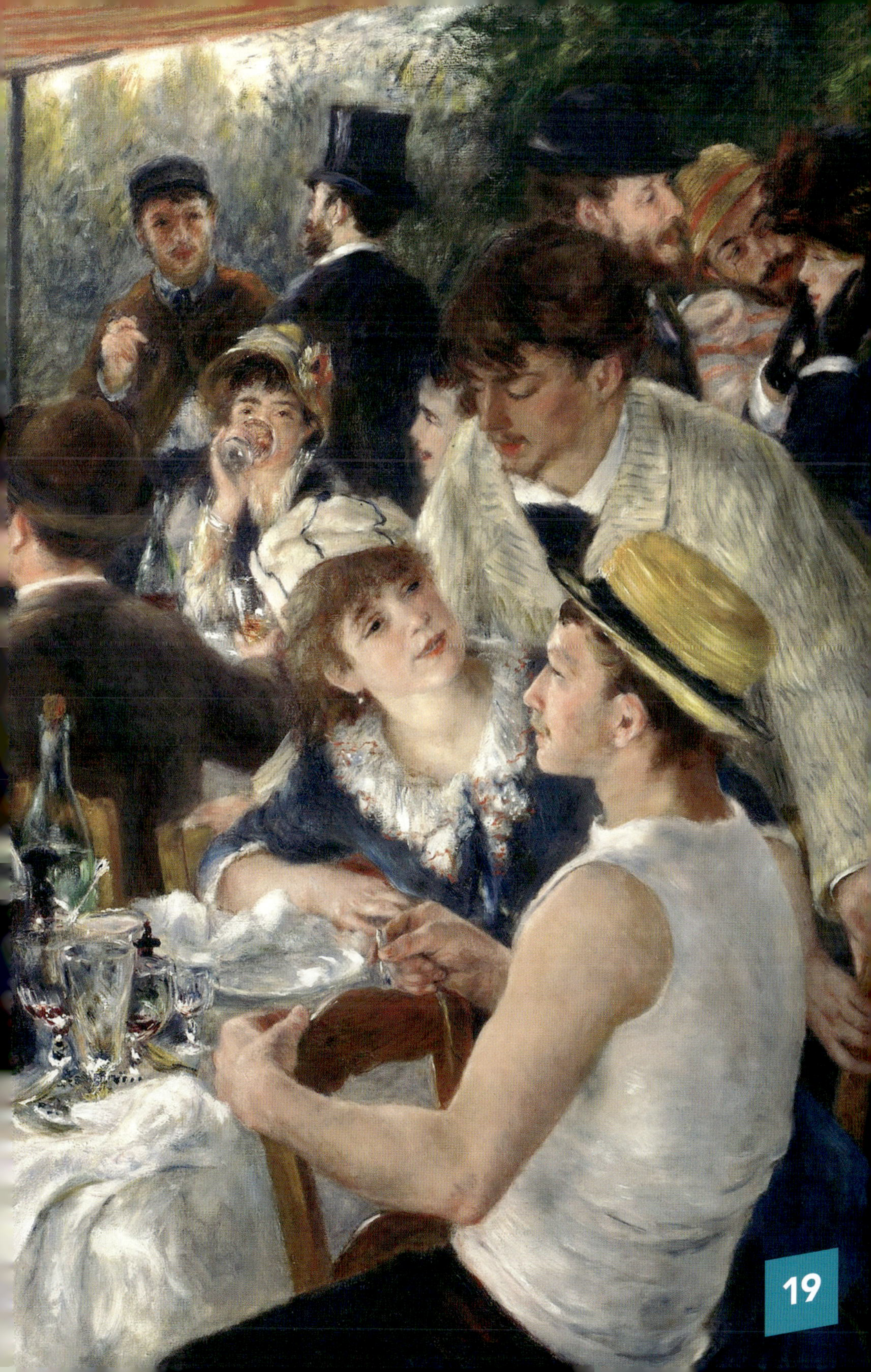

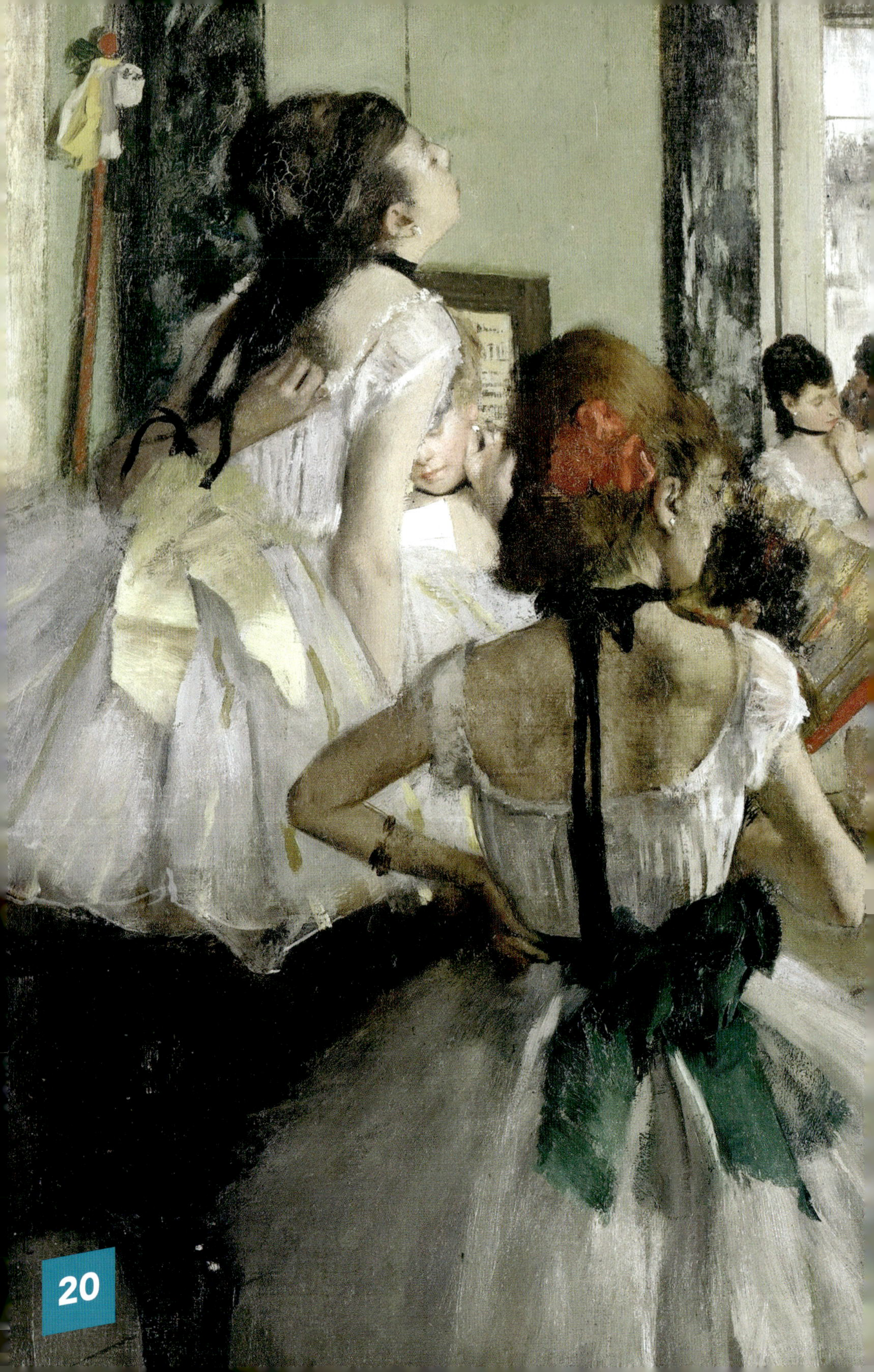

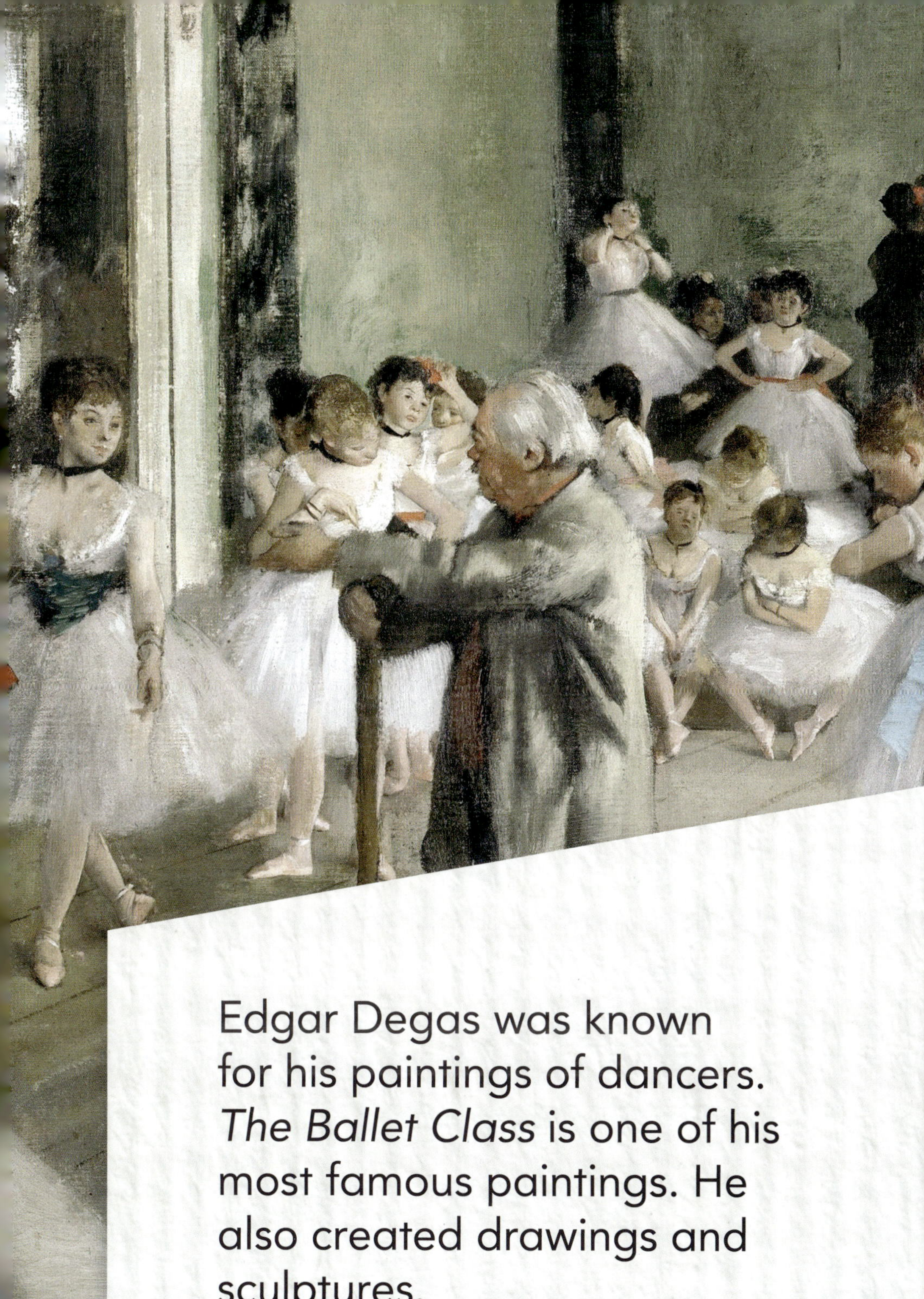

Edgar Degas was known for his paintings of dancers. *The Ballet Class* is one of his most famous paintings. He also created drawings and sculptures.

More Facts

- The first Impressionist **exhibition** took place in 1874. It displayed 165 works by 30 artists.
- Landscape paintings that are done outdoors are called plein-air paintings. Impressionist painters often went on outdoor trips together to paint.
- Mary Cassatt was the only official American Impressionist. She was born in Philadelphia, but lived most of her adult life in France. She was known for her paintings of women and children.

Glossary

critic – a person whose work is to judge and write opinions about music, movies, plays, art, and literature.

exhibition – a public showing of art.

oil paint – a thick type of paint with an oil base that is slow-drying.

Index

Ballet Class, The 21

classical paintings 7

colors 10

Degas, Edgar 21

France 5, 9

Impression, Sunrise 16

Impressionists 10, 12, 14, 16

Luncheon of the Boating Party 18

Monet, Claude 16

oils 14

Renoir, Pierre-Auguste 18

style 9

technique 10, 12, 14

Online Resources

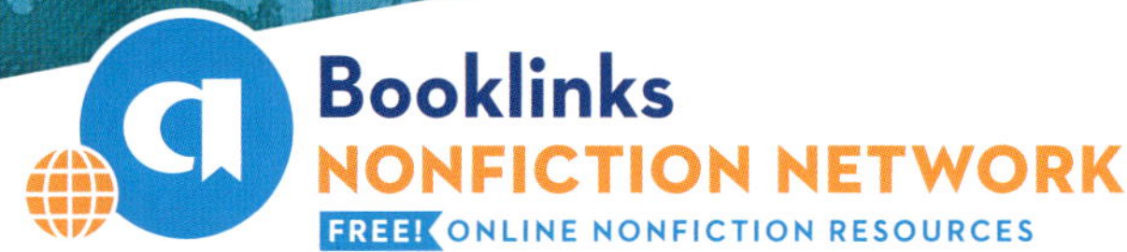

To learn more about Impressionism, please visit **abdobooklinks.com** or scan this QR code. These links are routinely monitored and updated to provide the most current information available.